reserves. Once the glycogen stores are depleted, the body draws on its protein stores, to the detriment of your muscle mass. Fat deposits are also drawn on for energy, but that does not result in as much power as the energy obtained from carbohydrates.

In a normal balanced diet, 55 per cent of the total energy content comes from carbo-hydrates. The body requires two to three days to replenish glycogen stores depleted by a workout or competition. The more you increase the carbohydrates in your diet (to 60–70 per cent), the faster you will regain that lost energy.

DRINK PLENTY OF WATER

You need to drink plenty of water on a regular basis. If you wait until you are thirsty, it's already too late: your body can no longer compensate adequately for the loss of fluids, and your performance is compromised. You should drink at least 1/2 litre (1 pt) water (ideally water rich in magnesium) before even beginning a workout. If your workout lasts longer than 45 minutes you should drink fluids while you are working out as well. A mixture of apple juice and mineral water is a good option since the minerals and carbohydrates give you additional stamina.

PROTEIN NEEDS

It is commonly held that athletes need more protein to build strength, but that is not the case. Just 0.8 grams of protein per kilogram of body weight per day (0.9 oz per stone) are more than sufficient. Only athletes participating in strength sports, such as weight-lifting, need more protein in accordance with their higher body weight. An excess of unused protein is converted into fat and ends up as fat deposits in undesirable locations. You do not need to buy expensive products from a chemists' or health food shop to find high-quality sources of protein. You can find such sources in common foods: for example, lean meat, poultry and fish, potatoes with an egg and quark, or beans and pulses with grains.

FAT, BUT NOT TOO MUCH FAT

Athletes should ideally eat a low-fat diet. Too much fat, especially from animal products, puts a strain on the body. Too little or no fat at all would be just as damaging. The following rule of thumb applies: fat should make up no more than 30 per cent of your total energy consumption per day.

Fat may include butter or margarine on your toast, high-quality olive oil on your salad, and fish two or three times a week. Cold-water fish, such as salmon, herring, or mackerel, contains the omega-3 fatty acids so important for your body.

The right thing at

Nutritious snacks for optimal performance

the right time

TO START OFF YOUR DAY

Always eat breakfast, regardless of whether you plan to work out on a given day. Breakfast is essential for giving you that extra edge needed by more than just your muscles – your brain profits as well. Without breakfast, your glycogen stores are half empty and continue to drain throughout the morning. A midday low is already pre-programmed. So always kick off your day with a hearty portion of carbohydrates. This may mean that you have to change your habits a bit, but the 15 minutes you need for a quick meal in the morning will pay off and enhance your mood all day long.

BEFORE YOUR WORKOUT

Shortly before your workout, you should ensure that your glycogen stores are topped up to optimum levels. You can do this by eating a small carbohydrate-rich snack. Bananas are an excellent choice – the quintessential fruit for athletes. Foods rich in fat or protein are not such a good choice, as these meals are digested slowly and reduce your performance.

DURING A WORKOUT

If you work out for longer than 45 minutes, you should always have fluids on hand. It is not a good idea to eat during a workout since solids put an additional strain on your body's digestion. The exception to this is if you are out on an all-day hike or playing tennis for hours. But even in these cases small snacks little and often, such as a cereal or fruit bar or a piece of fruit, are sufficient to replenish your glycogen stores. It is far more important that you drink fluids to replace the water you lose through perspiration. If your workout is strenuous or the weather is hot, an isotonic sports drink is better than plain water as it contains small amounts of sugar and sodium, which speed the rate that water reaches the tissues. To make your own isotonic drink mix fruit juice 50:50 with water. You should always avoid taking alcoholic drinks to quench your thirst. Although beer does contain minerals and carbohydrates, the alcohol content impairs their absorption, has a diuretic effect, and impedes the replenishment of glycogen stores.

Energy for
for more stamina, conditioning, and performance
sports and fitness

WHAT MAKES ATHLETES FIT?

One thing is obvious: if you exercise several times a week, you need more energy – regardless of whether you ride a bike, swim, walk, play tennis, or jog. You can and should eat more. Yet that fact does not give you carte blanche to fill up on anything you want with the excuse that it will be "worked off" while you exercise. On the contrary: only properly fed muscles will give you true power and an optimal workout.

CARBOHYDRATES, CARBOHYDRATES, AND MORE CARBOHYDRATES!

Carbohydrates are what give you strength and stamina. They are like tanking up with super-grade petrol for your muscles. Carbohydrates are also the best source of energy for nerves and the brain. Carbohydrates are converted into glycogen by your body and stored in your liver and muscles. Your muscles draw on this glycogen during a workout. Yet only about 240–500 grams of glycogen are stored in the liver and muscles. That is equivalent to about 1,000 to 2,000 kcal. During high-performance activities and endurance sports, your body needs to draw on its

ALWAYS EAT AFTER A WORKOUT

After an intensive workout you may not feel hungry for about an hour. Only after your metabolism and circulation return to normal will you feel hunger signals from your body. Yet your body is crying out for carbohydrates since its stores are considerably depleted from your efforts. The glycogen stores in your muscles are empty, and they need carbohydrates immediately, otherwise muscle cells will be broken down instead of being built up again. Starting on page 35, you will find recipes for meals ideal for replenishing your reserves.

Your body is also weakened from the huge efforts it has expended during a workout. This leaves the field open to free radicals, making it easy for these by-products of metabolism to attack the cells in your body. Antioxidant vitamins C and E are helpful in preventing this from happening. Fruits, fresh vegetables, and fruit and vegetable juices are a great source of vitamin C. When you perspire, you lose valuable minerals as well as water. Magnesium, potassium, and calcium are the minerals you lose in the greatest quantities, which is why it is especially important that the snack you eat after a workout and any fluids you drink should contain these minerals.

Ingredients

Power from natural sources

for fitness

FOODS WITH IMPACT

Apricots: A source of B vitamins, carotenoids, potassium, these small fruits are packed full of ingredients for fitness. In the winter months, dried unsulphured apricots make just as healthy a snack as the fresh fruit.

Bananas: A fruit custom-made for athletes. Bananas contain magnesium, potassium, beta carotene, biotin, and vitamin C, and they also give you just the right amount of carbohydrates for added stamina.

Fish: You should eat fish two to three times a week. Fish is a particularly valuable source of polyunsaturated fatty acids. Cold-water fish such as herring or mackerel is rich in essential omega-3 fatty acids.

Oats or oat bran: A good source of vitamins B1 and E as well as the minerals calcium and magnesium. Even small amounts provide plenty of carbohydrates.

Beans and pulses: These contain vitamins and minerals, and are a highly nutritious source of protein and carbohydrate.

Redcurrants: An important source of flavonoid antioxidants and vitamin C; they are a great aid in achieving overall fitness.

Seed oils: A source of polyunsaturates of the omega-6 family, in particular linoleic acid. Polyunsaturated fatty acids are essential to life. Eat 1–2 tablespoons per day.

Cress: A great source of magnesium and potassium; also contains vitamin C, and carotenoids.

Carrots: As a raw snack, as juice, or grated in a salad, carrots give a quick energy boost. Cooked carrots are rich in beta carotene.

Seeds and nuts: A source of magnesium, potassium, omega-6 fatty acids, and an extra dose of vitamin E. Try sprinkling them over a salad or on your breakfast cereal.

Rice and wild rice: A good source of energy and energy-giving B vitamins.

Beetroot: Contains potassium and also the blood-fortifying mineral iron.

Dried fruits: Good sources of all minerals, dried fruits are an essential component of fitness nutrition. A better choice of snack than chocolate or cake!

Whole grain products: A must for active sportspeople, if only for the complex carbohydrates they offer. They also supply all minerals and nearly all vitamins.

Substance	Important for	Found in	Daily needs
Magnesium	Muscle activity, nerves, enzymes, cell energy, hormone transportation, immune system, mineral utilization, heart function	Whole grain products, beans and pulses, milk, green vegetables, potatoes, mineral water	300–350 mg
Potassium	Nerve impulses, cell metabolism, enzymes, supply of oxygen to the brain, fluid balance, carbohydrate metabolism, heart beat	Fruit, dried fruits, potatoes, and other vegetables	3–4 g
Vitamin E (Tocopherol)	Nerves, muscles, skin, circulation, fat metabolism, protects cells from free radicals	Vegetable oils, particularly seed oils, peas, nuts, avocado	12 mg
Vitamin B1 (Thiamin)	Processing of carbohydrates, transmission of nerve stimuli, activation of magnesium	Beans and pulses, whole grain bread, potatoes, poultry, liver	1.1–1.5 mg
Vitamin B2 (Riboflavin)	Protein and carbohydrate metabolism, skin	Milk products, meat, fish, eggs, whole grain bread	1.8 mg
Vitamin B12	Formation of red blood cells (together with iron), activates enzymes for provision of muscle energy	Liver, fish, eggs, and milk products	5 mcg = .005 mg
Niacin	Energy release in cells, healthy nervous system	Whole grain bread, beef, poultry, salmon, yeast	15–20 mg
Biotin (Vitamin H)	Synthesis of carbohydrates and fatty acids, energy supply, nervous system, skin, hair, nails	Offal, milk, soya beans, whole grain bread, lentils, chicken liver	0.03–0.1 mg
Vitamin C (Ascorbic acid)	Iron utilization, immune system, blood formation, blood vessels	Peppers, tomatoes, cauliflower, citrus fruits, broccoli, redcurrants	75 mg
Beta carotene	Immune system	Orange-coloured fruits and vegetables, green vegetables, tomatoes	Not known
Iron	Transportation of oxygen in the blood, muscle tissues, heart function, hormone metabolism	Beef and other red meat, lentils with vegetables, whole grain bread with fruit	10–15 mg

The daily requirements of magnesium, potassium, vitamin E and vitamin C may be double for those participating in intense sports activities.

Power
Vitamins and minerals you can enjoy
week

EVERYDAY FITNESS

This weekly plan gives you a sample meal plan for days you work out. But feel free to enjoy these meals every day of the week – they are low in fat and high in fitness. On the days you don't work out, simply enjoy the before and after workout snacks whenever you like, or replace them with a piece of fruit.

PLENTY OF CARBOHYDRATES

We have designed each day so you consume approximately 200 g of pure carbohydrates. Depending on your training regime, you can increase your carbohydrates on particularly intense days by adding bananas, more rice, or a larger portion of bread.

PLENTY OF MAGNESIUM

Athletes cannot meet their daily magnesium requirements through solid food alone. That's why it's particularly important that you make sure the mineral water you drink is a good source of magnesium (at least 100 mg per litre or 50 mg per pint, just look on the label).

FITNESS YOU CAN DRINK

The drinks in the recipe section are a powerhouse of nutrition! You can drink them throughout the day or before a workout. They do not have enough carbohydrates to replace a meal after a workout, but they make a good aperitif before your main meal of the day.

PURE NATURE INSTEAD OF BOTTLED CONCOCTIONS

In theory you could get all the vitamins and minerals you need from supplements. But your body can absorb and use these nutrients much more efficiently when they are delivered in small amounts throughout the day instead of in just one large dose once a day. In addition, food has a wealth of phytochemicals and bioactive components which aren't vitamins and minerals and can't be found in a pill. If you plan your meals carefully, your body can get everything it needs without supplements.

WEEKLY PLAN

Monday

* Breakfast: Rice flakes with peaches
* Before: 2 Herb muffins with ham ❈ After: Pancakes with dried fruit
* Herb-coated pike-perch fillet ❈ Drink: Deep purple athletes' drink

Tuesday

* Breakfast: Avocado cream on spelt bread
* Before: 2 Muffins with cornflakes ❈ After: Butter bean salad with celery
* Turkey schnitzel in coconut milk ❈ Drink: Mango, yogurt, and orange smoothie

Wednesday

* Breakfast: Shrimps on rye bread ❈ Before: 2 Banana muffins with hazelnuts
* After: Serrano ham with mushrooms
* Spaghetti with courgettes and steak ❈ Drink: Sweet apricot dream

Thursday

* Breakfast: Bananas and Galia melon❈ Before: Mango, yogurt, and orange smoothie ❈ After: Tuna cream on whole grain toast
* Pork fillet in persimmon sauce ❈ Drink: Papaya and pineapple milk

Friday

* Breakfast: Orange and almond muesli with figs
* Before: Bean tapenade with leeks ❈ After: Mango and redcurrant salad
* Chicken breast and apricot ragout ❈ Drink: Hot pepper milk

Saturday

* Breakfast: Parma ham with cottage cheese ❈ Before: Cheese and cucumber sandwich ❈ After: Couscous with sweetcorn and sage
* Swordfish and mango goulash ❈ Drink: Melon mix with redcurrants

Sunday

* Breakfast: Mango muesli
* Before: Honeydew melon with figs ❈ After: Fennel and pineapple
* Leek-wrapped salmon steaks ❈ Drink: Yellow pepper and carrot mix

Shrimps on

rich in vitamins and minerals

rye bread

Serves 2: • 50 g (2 oz) low-fat quark • 4 tbsp low-fat yogurt • salt • pepper
• 4 slices rye bread • 2 tbsp chopped chives • 1 star fruit • 125 g (5 oz) cooked and
peeled shrimps • 1 sprig of dill

Stir together the quark, yogurt, salt, and pepper. Spread two slices of rye bread
with half this mixture, then sprinkle with chives. Top each with another slice
of rye bread and then spread with the remaining mixture.

Cut the star fruit in half crosswise and slice off two "stars". Dice the remaining
star fruit, then mix with the shrimps and spoon on top of both sandwiches.
Wash the dill, shake off excess moisture, then pinch off the leaves and sprinkle
over the top. Garnish with the star fruit stars and serve.

power

PER SERVING: 217 kcal • 20 g protein • 3 g fat • 29 g carbohydrate

Mango
rich in vitamin E, potassium, and magnesium
muesli

Serves 2: • 25 g (1 oz) rye flakes • 1/8 l (1/4 pt) low-fat milk • 1 tbsp crème fraîche

• 2 tbsp sunflower seeds • 1 mango

Pour the milk over the rye flakes, then stir in the crème fraîche and allow to stand for

10 minutes. Toast the sunflower seeds in an unoiled non-stick pan. Peel the mango, cut the fruit

from the stone, dice, and fold into the flakes. Sprinkle with toasted sunflower seeds and serve.

power

PER SERVING: 257 kcal • 7 g protein • 10 g fat • 34 g carbohydrate

Orange and almond
rich in magnesium and potassium
muesli with figs

Serves 2: • 50 g (2 oz) dried figs • 3 tbsp rolled oats • 1/8 l (1/4 pt) low-fat milk • 1 orange

• 25 g (1 oz) flaked almonds • 150 ml (5 fl oz) low-fat yogurt • pinch of cinnamon

Finely chop the figs, then combine with the oats and milk in a bowl and allow to stand for

5 minutes. Peel and dice the orange. Toast the flaked almonds in an unoiled non-stick pan. Fold

the diced oranges and yogurt into the muesli. Sprinkle with the hot almonds and dust with

cinnamon before serving.

power

PER SERVING: 262 kcal • 10 g protein • 10 g fat • 36 g carbohydrate

Rice flakes

rich in carbohydrates and magnesium

with peaches

Serves 2: • 300 ml (1/2 pt) low-fat milk • 2 tbsp raw cane sugar • 100 g (4 oz) rice flakes (health food

shop) • 3 peaches (approx 300 g (12 oz))• 1 tbsp pistachio nuts • 2 tbsp raisins • 2 tbsp cornflakes

Heat the milk and the sugar, then pour the mixture over the rice flakes, cover, and allow to

stand for 10 minutes. Pour boiling water over the peaches, then peel and dice them. Chop the

pistachio nuts and toast them in an unoiled non-stick pan. Gently fold the diced peaches and

raisins into the rice flakes. Sprinkle with the cornflakes and pistachios and serve.

power

PER SERVING: 384 kcal • 8 g protein • 4 g fat • 80 g carbohydrate

Bananas

for increased muscle performance

and Galia melon

Serves 2: • 2 bananas • 5 tbsp oat bran • 2 tsp mango chutney

• 1/2 Galia melon (approx 300 g (12 oz)) • 2 tbsp pine nuts

Mash the bananas with a fork, then stir in the oat bran and mango chutney. Remove the melon

seeds and peel and cut the fruit into pieces. Stir the melon into the banana mixture. Chop the

pine nuts, toast them in an unoiled non-stick pan, and sprinkle over the fruit.

power

PER SERVING: 275 kcal • 5 g protein • 6 g fat • 53 g carbohydrate

Parma ham
with Honeydew melon and tomato juice
with cottage cheese

Remove the seeds and peel from the melon and cut the fruit into very

small cubes. In a bowl mix the cottage cheese into the diced melon and

Serves 2:
1/4 Honeydew melon
(approx. 150 g (6 oz))
100 g (4 oz) cottage cheese
salt
pepper
2 wholewheat bread rolls
50 g (2 oz) Parma ham, sliced
paper-thin
300 ml (1/2 pt) tomato juice

add salt and pepper to taste.

Cut the bread rolls in half and spread each half

with the melon and cottage cheese mixture. Cut

any fat from the Parma ham, roll each slice loosely

and arrange on the rolls. Season with freshly

ground white pepper to taste.

A glass of tomato juice rounds out the meal.

Tomato juice

Lycopene, the substance that gives tomatoes their
bright red colour, has been shown to slow down free
radicals in the body. And the good news is, lycopene
remains in tomato products even after processing –
in tomato juice, for example. In fact heating lycopene
actually makes it easier for the body to use.

PER SERVING:

240 kcal

18 g protein

3 g fat

34 g carbohydrate

power

Red grapefruit

with Amaretti – small Italian macaroons

and prunes

Serves 2: • 1 red grapefruit • 5 tbsp wheatgerm • 10 pitted prunes (approx. 50 g (2 oz))

• 150 g (6 oz) low-fat yogurt • 10 Amaretti

Carefully peel and section the grapefruit, taking care to catch any juice. Mix the grapefruit segments, juice, and wheatgerm in a bowl. Cut the prunes into strips and fold them into the grapefruit and wheatgerm mixture together with the yogurt. Spoon into dessert glasses. Crush the Amaretti, sprinkle the crumbs over, and serve.

PER SERVING: 146 kcal • 6 g protein • 2 g fat • 25 g carbohydrate

Camembert cream

also good as a snack

on rye bread

Serves 2: • 50 g (2 oz) ripe Camembert (30% fat) • 100 g (4 oz) low-fat quark

• 1–2 tbsp low-fat milk • salt • white pepper • 1/2 tsp sweet paprika • 2 spring onions

• 4 slices rye bread • 2 tbsp chopped chives

Cut the Camembert into small pieces, cut off the rind, then purée with the quark and milk. Season with salt, pepper, and paprika. Wash and trim the spring onions, then cut them in half lengthways before chopping finely. Stir the chopped spring onions into the Camembert cream and spread the mixture on to the slices of bread, garnishing with chives.

PER SERVING: 235 kcal • 18 g protein • 5 g fat • 31 g carbohydrate

Avocado cream
with cress and strawberries
on spelt bread

Cut the avocado in half and remove the stone. Using a spoon, scoop out the flesh of the avocado, place in a bowl, and mash coarsely with a fork. Mix in the salt, pepper, and raspberry vinegar. Lightly toast the slices of bread, then spread the avocado mixture on each slice. Using scissors, carefully cut the cress and sprinkle over the avocado. Wash and hull the strawberries, then cut into slices. Arrange the strawberries on the bread slices, and season to taste with freshly ground pepper.

Serves 2:
1 small avocado (250–300 g (10–12 oz))
salt
black pepper
2 tbsp raspberry vinegar
4 slices spelt bread (approx. 50 g (2 oz) each)
1 box cress
4 strawberries (approx. 60 g (2 oz))

Avocado

Avocados boast the highest natural fat content of all fruits and vegetables. Three-quarters of their fat content consists of easily digested polyunsaturated fats. Avocados are also a rich source of biotin, which controls energy production in the muscles. In addition, biotin positively affects the protein metabolism of skin, hair, and nails, which is why avocados are considered a beauty fruit.

PER SERVING:

240 kcal

7 g protein

8 g fat

33 g carbohydrate

Mango, yogurt,

terrific source of magnesium and potassium

and orange smoothie

Finely chop the sunflower seeds, toast in an unoiled non-stick pan until their aroma is released, then set aside to cool. Peel the mango and separate the flesh from the stone in wedges, taking care to catch any juice in a bowl. Set aside two mango wedges for a garnish. Juice the orange and the lime halves. Purée the mango together with the orange and lime juice, the oat bran, water, and yogurt in a blender. Fill two glasses and sprinkle with the toasted sunflower seeds. Garnish with a wedge of mango on the rim of each glass and serve the drinks immediately.

Serves 2:
1 tbsp sunflower seeds
1 ripe mango (approx. 300 g (12 oz))
1 orange
1/2 lime
2 tbsp oat bran
125 ml (4 fl oz) yogurt
125 ml (4 fl oz) water

Mango – a favourite fruit through the ages

Mangos are believed to have been cultivated in India over 6,000 years ago and are a symbol of strength and power. That's not surprising since they are a rich source of beta carotene, vitamins, and minerals. They can now be found nearly everywhere and can be used in a variety of ways, even as a side dish for meat or fish.

PER SERVING:

240 kcal

7 g protein

8 g fat

33 g carbohydrate

Deep purple
athletes' drink

with beetroot for peak energy

Serves 2: • 2 beetroot (approx. 200 g (8 oz) each) • 2 small apples • 2 medium carrots

• juice from 1/2 lemon • 2 tsp horseradish • celery salt • white pepper

Wash and peel the beetroot, then cut into eight (wear gloves to prevent your hands from staining). Wash, quarter, and core the apples. Wash the carrots. Put the beetroot, apples, and carrots into a juicer. Mix the juice with the lemon juice and horseradish. Season to taste with the celery salt and pepper.

power

PER SERVING: 92 kcal • 2 g protein • 1 g fat • 21 g carbohydrate

Sweet apricot
dream

rich in potassium for peak performance

Serves 2: • 500 g (1lb 4 oz) ripe apricots • 1 lime • 2 red grapefruits • 1 tbsp raw cane sugar

• mineral water • 2 mint leaves

Wash, stone, and juice the apricots. Cut the lime and grapefruits in half. Squeeze the juice from one lime half and the grapefruits. Moisten the rims of the glasses with water and dip in the sugar. Mix the apricot, grapefruit, and lime juices, pour into the glasses, then fill with mineral water. Garnish the drinks with slices of the remaining lime half and mint leaves.

power

PER SERVING: 140 kcal • 3 g protein • 1 g fat • 30 g carbohydrate

Green

for immediate energy

pick-me-up

Serves 2: • 200 g (8 oz) cucumber • 2 kiwi fruit • 3 sprigs dill • 1/4 l (1/2 pt) buttermilk

• 1/2 tsp cumin • salt • pepper • mineral water

Peel the cucumber and the kiwi fruit. Wash the dill, shake dry, and remove the leaves from the stem. Purée the cucumber, kiwi fruit, buttermilk, and dill in a blender. Season with the cumin, salt, and pepper. Let the mixture stand for several minutes before pouring it into the glasses and filling to the top with mineral water.

PER SERVING: 45 kcal • 11 g protein • 1 g fat • 8 g carbohydrate

Yellow

refreshing and rich in magnesium

secret

Serves 2: • 1 pineapple (approx. 300 g (12 oz)) • 1 banana • 5 sprigs mint

• 1/4 l (1/2 pt) buttermilk • 2 tbsp maple syrup • 1 tbsp linseed

Peel the pineapple and slice it into quarters lengthways. Remove the hard inner core and cut the pineapple into pieces. Peel the banana. Remove the mint leaves from the stems and set several aside. Purée the pineapple, banana, mint leaves, and buttermilk in a blender. Mix in the maple syrup and linseed. Chop the remaining mint leaves. Serve in glasses garnished with mint.

PER SERVING: 188 kcal • 2 g protein • 2 g fat • 43g carbohydrate

Melon mix

particularly rich in minerals

with redcurrants

Wash the redcurrants and set aside two sprigs as a garnish; remove the remaining redcurrants from the stems. Cut the melon in half and scoop out the seeds. Cut one melon half into wedges and remove the peel, then chop into 1 cm (1/2 in) cubes. Purée the redcurrants, melon, honey, and buttermilk in a blender.

Moisten the rims of the glasses with water and dip into the sugar. Pour the drink into glasses, garnish with a sprig of redcurrants, and serve immediately.

Serves 2:
100 g (4 oz) redcurrants
1/2 Honeydew melon
(approx. 350 g (14 oz))
1 tsp wildflower honey
1/8 l (1/4 pt) buttermilk
2 tsp raw cane sugar

Redcurrants – an energy powerhouse

Redcurrants are an outstanding source of beta carotene, B vitamins, and vitamin C. On top of that, they are packed with potassium and calcium. These small berries are an energy powerhouse and are delicious eaten as a snack or combined with quark or yogurt.

PER SERVING:

157 kcal

4 g protein

1 g fat

33 g carbohydrate

Hot

for fans of spicy drinks

pepper milk

Serves 2: • 2 tbsp sesame seeds • 2 red peppers • 4 vine-ripened tomatoes

• salt • pepper • dash of Tabasco sauce • 300 ml (1/2 pt) ice-cold low-fat milk

Toast the sesame seeds in an unoiled non-stick pan until they are golden brown, then set aside.
Cut the peppers in half, wash, and remove the stems, seeds, and inner membranes. Wash the
tomatoes, then cut in half and remove the stems. Put the tomatoes and peppers into a juicer.
Season with salt, pepper, and Tabasco sauce. Pour the juice into glasses and add the milk.
Garnish with sesame seeds.

PER SERVING: 128 kcal• 6 g protein • 5 g fat • 17 g carbohydrate

Celery and yellow

promotes circulation and metabolism

pepper powerhouse

Serves 2: • 450 g (1 lb) celery • 2 yellow peppers • cayenne pepper • 2 lemon balm leaves and

1 tbsp chopped lemon balm • 1 tsp rock salt • mineral water

Wash the celery. Cut the pepper in half, remove the stem, seeds, and inner membranes. Juice the
celery and the pepper, then season the juice with cayenne pepper. Mix the chopped lemon balm
with the salt and spread the mixture on a plate. Moisten the rims of the glasses with water and
dip into the salt and lemon balm mixture. Pour the juice into the glasses, add the desired
amount of mineral water, and garnish with the lemon balm leaves.

PER SERVING: 70 kcal• 4 g protein • 1 g fat • 13 g carbohydrate

Papaya and pineapple milk

particularly high in potassium and beta carotene

Serves 2: • 1 papaya • 1 small pineapple • juice from 1/2 lime • 200 ml low-fat milk

• mineral water • 1 tbsp dessicated coconut

Cut the papaya in half, remove the stone, and scoop out the flesh with a spoon. Peel the pineapple, taking care to cut out any brown spots. Slice off two thin sections and set aside, then cut the remaining pineapple into small pieces. Purée the pineapple in a blender together with the papaya, lime juice, and milk. Add the mineral water. Moisten the rims of the glasses and dip into the coconut. Serve the drink in glasses garnished with pineapple slices.

Per serving: 161 kcal• 3 g protein • 3 g fat • 31 g carbohydrate

Yellow pepper and carrot mix

with a dash of oil to promote vitamin A absorption

Serves 2: • 1 yellow pepper • 2 kohlrabi • 500 g (1lb 4oz) carrots • 2 tsp chopped parsley

• celery salt • 2 drops wheatgerm oil

Cut the pepper in half, wash, and remove the stem, seeds and inner membranes. Peel the kohlrabi and carrots. Run the vegetables through a juicer. Season the juice to taste with parsley and celery salt. Pour into two glasses, stir in 1 drop of wheatgerm oil to each glass and serve immediately.

Per serving: 104 kcal• 5 g protein • 1 g fat • 19 g carbohydrate

Herb muffins
a hearty snack for people on-the-go
with ham

Preheat the oven to 200°C (400°F). Clean and finely dice the shallots. Cut about 50 g (2 oz) of the ham into small cubes. Heat the oil in a non-stick pan. Sauté the shallots and diced ham until crispy, then set aside.

Put the quark, milk, egg, salt, pepper, and Gouda cheese in a bowl and mix well. Sift the flour into this mixture. Mix in the sugar and baking powder. Fold in the shallot and ham mixture, parsley, and thyme.

Lightly oil the muffin pans, then spoon in the batter. Cut the remaining ham into strips and arrange in a criss-cross pattern over the tops of the muffins. Bake the muffins in the middle of the preheated oven for about 20–25 minutes, until they are golden brown. Leave on a wire rack to cool.

Makes 12 muffins:

2 shallots
75 g (3 oz) lean cooked ham
2 tbsp vegetable oil
150 g (6 oz) low-fat quark
50–75 ml (1–2 fl oz) milk
1 egg
salt
pepper
2 tbsp grated Gouda cheese
200 g (7 oz) rye flour
1/2 tsp sugar
2 tsp baking powder
3 tbsp chopped parsley
1 tbsp chopped thyme
oil for the muffin pans

▶ Good things come in small packages

Muffins come from the United States and are the latest trend. Whether simple or sophisticated, sweet or spicy, as a snack or part of a meal – muffins are always popular. They taste best when they are fresh and still slightly warm. Muffins can also be frozen and reheated when required.

PER MUFFIN:

108 kcal

6 g protein

4 g fat

13 g carbohydrate

power

Honeydew
rich in potassium and vitamin C
melon with figs

Serves 2: • 2 ripe figs • juice of 1/2 lime • 1 tbsp raw cane sugar

• 1/2 Honeydew melon • 2 tbsp mascarpone cheese • mint leaves

Dice the figs. Stir together the lime juice and sugar, add the diced figs, and marinate for 10 minutes. Scoop out the seeds from the melon, remove the peel, cut the melon into pieces, then purée. Beat the mascarpone cheese until creamy, then fold in to the melon purée. Add the diced figs and marinade, then refrigerate for one hour. Garnish with mint leaves and serve.

PER SERVING: 113 kcal • 1 g protein • 3 g fat • 20 g carbohydrate

Rice cakes
ultra light and refreshing
with redcurrants

Serves 2: • 75 g (3 oz) redcurrants • 1 tsp agave or maple syrup (health food shop) • 1 tbsp cottage cheese

• 2 tbsp low-fat yogurt • black pepper • 2 rice cakes • thyme leaves

Remove the redcurrants from the stems and place in bowl. Crush them lightly with a fork and drizzle with the agave syrup. Blend the cottage cheese with the yogurt until smooth, then season with pepper. Fold in the redcurrants, then spoon the mixture on to the rice cakes and garnish with thyme leaves.

PER SERVING: 119 kcal • 1 g protein • 1 g fat • 26 g carbohydrate

Banana muffins

bursting with carbohydrates for immediate energy

with hazelnuts

Preheat the oven to 200°C (400°F). Use an electric mixer to cream the honey, margarine, and eggs in a bowl for 5 minutes until light and foamy. Peel and mash the bananas. Add the mashed bananas, hazelnuts, and vanilla essence to the margarine mixture and beat for another 2 minutes until creamy. Sift together the flour and baking powder, then add to the mixture and stir in thoroughly.

Lightly oil the muffin pans and spoon in the batter. Take care to fill the pans to only two-thirds capacity since the batter will rise. Sprinkle the tops of the muffins with raisins.

Bake the muffins in the middle of the preheated oven for about 20 minutes until golden brown. Let them cool for a while in the pans before lightly brushing them with maple syrup.

Makes 12:
100 g (4 oz) honey
125 g (5 oz) low-fat margarine
2 eggs
2 bananas
50 g (2 oz) ground hazelnuts
1 tsp vanilla essence
225 g (9 oz) wholewheat flour
2 tsp baking powder
oil for the muffin pans
20 g (1 oz) raisins
2 tbsp maple syrup

> **Bananas**

Bananas are the ideal fruit for athletes! Whether incorporated in a dish or simply eaten plain after a workout, bananas give you the carbohydrate kick you need. A great source of potassium and magnesium, they can help replenish your mineral stores. And niacin promotes improved energy acquisition.

PER SERVING:

193 kcal

4 g protein

8 g fat

26 g carbohydrate

power

Muffins
a portable source of magnesium
with cornflakes

Preheat the oven to 200°C (400 °F). Cut the apricots into thin strips. Clean, peel, and grate the carrots. Mix the grated carrot with the eggs and honey. Stir in the raisins, apricots, almonds, and orange zest.

Mix together the flour and baking powder in a bowl. Sift the flour mixture into the other ingredients and stir until a stiff batter is formed.

Lightly oil the muffin pans and spoon 1 tablespoon of batter into each, smoothing the mixture flat. Bake in the middle of the preheated oven for about 20 minutes until golden brown.

While the muffins are baking, warm the apricot jam and water slowly in a small pot until the jam melts. Leave the muffins to cool slightly on a wire rack. Then brush them with the apricot jam mixture, and sprinkle the cornflakes over.

Makes 12:
8 dried apricots
2 medium-sized carrots
2 eggs
4 tbsp honey
25 g (1 oz) raisins
50 g (2 oz) chopped almonds
zest from 1/2 unwaxed orange
150 g (6 oz) wholewheat flour
2 tsp baking powder
oil for the muffin pans
For the garnish:
2 tbsp apricot jam
2 tbsp water
25 g (1 oz) cornflakes

PER MUFFIN: 131 kcal • 4 g protein • 4 g fat • 21 g carbohydrate

Bean tapenade

also good as an appetizer and for guests

with leeks

Trim the leek and the carrot. Cut the leek in half lengthways, wash, then slice crossways into half rings. Peel the carrot and cut into slices. Heat the olive oil in a non-stick pan. Lightly sauté the vegetables over a low heat, stirring constantly. Add the vegetable stock and cook over a low heat for about 10–15 minutes until the stock has evaporated and the vegetables are al dente.

Drain the kidney beans, then purée them with the herbs, capers, leek, and carrot. Season the tapenade to taste with salt and pepper, then refrigerate.

This bean tapenade is a tasty dip for raw vegetables, but also works well as a spread for whole grain bread. It keeps well for up to a week in the refrigerator.

Serves 3-4:
1 leek
1 medium-sized carrot
1 tbsp olive oil
1/8 l (4 fl oz) vegetable stock
1 small can kidney beans
(about 250 g (9 oz) drained)
1 tbsp chopped savory
1 tbsp chopped thyme
2 tsp capers
salt
pepper

Whole grains, beans, and pulses

The combination of whole grains with beans and pulses is of particular biological value. Combined in this way, the protein in beans and pulses can be ideally absorbed by the body. If you prefer to cut down on animal-based protein, this is a good source of the protein you need.

PER SERVING:

100 kcal

5 g protein

3 g fat

13 g carbohydrate

power

Cheese and

replenishes carbohydrate stores

cucumber sandwich

Spread the cottage cheese on the bread slices. Wash and peel the cucumber if necessary, then cut into thin slices. Arrange the cucumber slices on the cottage cheese. Use a sharp knife to cut the Romadur cheese into four thin slices. Arrange the cheese slices over the cucumber.

Trim and wash the spring onions, then slice finely. Mix the chives and spring onions together with the salt, pepper, and white wine vinegar. Stir in the wheatgerm oil.

Spoon this mixture over the open cheese sandwiches, then season to taste with freshly ground pepper.

Serves 2:

2 thick slices of rye bread

2 tbsp cottage cheese

100 g (4 oz) cucumber

100 g (4 oz) Romadur or Harzer cheese

2 spring onions

2 tbsp chopped chives

salt

freshly ground pepper

2 tbsp white wine vinegar

2 tsp wheatgerm oil

For more variety

You can make these sandwiches with the same amount of any other low-fat cheese. Also try using parsley, or other fresh herbs, instead of chives.

PER SERVING:

219 kcal

22 g protein

6 g fat

20 g carbohydrate

power

Pancakes with
with apricots and pineapple flakes
dried fruit

Cut the apricots into small cubes. Use a sharp knife to chop the pineapple flakes coarsely, then mix with the diced apricots. Add the milk and leave to stand for about 5 minutes.

Beat the egg in a bowl, then add in the fruit mixture. Sift the flour, then gradually stir it into the mixture. Let the batter stand for 2–3 minutes.

Heat 1 tsp butter in a small non-stick pan (about 20 cm (8 in) in diameter) and then fry the pancakes over a high heat until golden brown, using half the mixture each time. Spread 1 tsp soured cream over each pancake, then roll it up, sprinkle with pineapple flakes and serve with a glass of cold milk.

Serves 2:
25 g (1 oz) dried apricots (unsulphured)
25 g (1 oz) dried pineapple flakes
1/8 l (4 fl oz) low-fat milk
1 egg
50 g (2 oz) wholewheat flour
2 tsp butter
2 tsp soured cream

Dried fruit powerhouses
100 g (4 oz) dried figs contain 70 mg magnesium and are an excellent source of potassium. That's why figs – as well as other dried fruits – are strongly recommended as a part of an athlete's diet. Other outstanding choices include dried apricots and plums, pineapple flakes, and banana chips.

PER SERVING:
256 kcal
9 g protein
9 g fat
34 g carbohydrate

Couscous with

replenishes depleted magnesium levels

sweetcorn and sage

Serves 2: • 150 ml (1/4 pt) water • 100 g (4 oz) couscous • 2 tsp poppy seed oil • 1 small tin of sweetcorn

• 100 g (4 oz) mushrooms • 2 tbsp sage • 4 tbsp low-fat yogurt • 2 tbsp white balsamic vinegar

• salt • pepper

Bring the water to the boil and add the couscous, then stir in the oil and let the couscous stand for 10 minutes. Drain the sweetcorn. Clean the mushrooms and slice thinly. Cut the sage into strips and mix everything with the couscous. Combine the yogurt with the balsamic vinegar, salt, and pepper, and stir into the salad.

power

PER SERVING: 369 kcal • 12 g protein • 6 g fat • 68 g carbohydrate

Mango and redcurrant

also tasty with fresh peaches

salad

Serves 2: • 1 mango • 4 fresh apricots • 100 g (4 oz) redcurrants • juice from 1/2 lemon

• 30 g (1 oz) raw cane sugar • 2 tbsp oatmeal

Peel the mango and cut into small cubes. Wash the apricots, then cut them in half, remove the stones, and cut into thin wedges. Wash the redcurrants and remove from the stems. Mix the mango, apricots, and redcurrants together. Sprinkle with lemon juice and arrange on plates. Melt the sugar in a pan together with 2 tbsp water. Add the oatmeal and stir constantly until it browns, then pour over the fruit salad.

power

PER SERVING: 240 kcal • 3 g protein • 2 g fat • 51 g carbohydrate

Chicory salad
replenishes potassium and magnesium after a workout
with apricots

Blanch the apricots in hot water and remove the skins. Cut them in half, remove the stones, and cut into thin wedges. Coarsely chop the pumpkin seeds and toast in an unoiled non-stick pan and set aside to cool.

To prepare the marinade, mix together the maple syrup and balsamic vinegar in a bowl and season to taste with salt and pepper. Gradually beat in the oil with a balloon whisk. Add the apricot wedges and pumpkin seeds to the marinade and leave to stand for about 10 minutes.

Remove the outer leaves of the chicory, then cut the heads in half lengthways and remove the core. Cut the halves into 1 cm (1/2 in) wide strips and mix well with the apricots. Arrange the chicory salad on plates and serve.

Serves 2:
10 fresh apricots
(about 350 g(14 oz))
1 tbsp pumpkin seeds
1 tbsp maple syrup
2 tbsp balsamic vinegar
salt
pepper
2 tbsp pumpkin seed oil
2 small heads of chicory

37

Speciality oil from the Styria region of Austria

Pumpkin seed oil is derived from the black seeds of a native pumpkin (seeds are usually white). It is a very dark oil ("black gold") that should be used very sparingly. You should also be aware that this oil leaves stains that are very difficult to remove.

PER SERVING:
223 kcal
5 g protein
11 g fat
25 g carbohydrate

Butter bean salad
a wonderful source of magnesium
with celery

Empty the beans into a strainer, rinse with cold water, and drain. Peel the shallots and garlic. Dice the shallots and slice the garlic cloves.

Serves 2:
1 can butter beans
(250 g (9 oz) drained)
2 shallots
2 cloves garlic
1 tbsp olive oil
5 tbsp raspberry vinegar
salt
pepper
5 cherry tomatoes
1 stick celery
15 g (1/2 oz) walnuts
2 slices whole grain bread

For the dressing, heat the oil in a small non-stick pan. Add the shallots and garlic and sauté over medium heat until golden brown, then pour in the raspberry vinegar. Season the dressing with salt and pepper and mix with the beans while still warm.

Wash the cherry tomatoes and cut them in half. Wash and chop the celery. Mix the tomatoes and celery into the beans. Chop the walnuts. Arrange the salad, sprinkle with walnuts, and serve with whole grain bread.

38

▶ **Beans have it**

Red or white, dried or canned – in terms of nutrition for fitness fanatics, dried beans should be eaten frequently! One advantage: 100 g (4 oz) of dried beans contain 341 mg potassium and 39 mg magnesium, and a high percentage of carbohydrates. Canned beans offer only slightly fewer nutrients.

PER SERVING:

334 kcal

13 g protein

13 g fat

39 g carbohydrate

Serrano ham

also tastes good with other cured meats

with mushrooms

Serves 2: • 50 g (2 oz) mushrooms • 1 tsp lemon juice • 50 g (2 oz) Serrano ham • 4 tbsp cottage cheese • 2 tbsp chopped chives • 2 thick slices wholewheat bread • freshly ground black pepper

Clean the mushrooms, chop finely, and sprinkle with lemon juice. Discard any fat from the ham, cut the ham into small pieces, and mix with the mushrooms. Fold in the cottage cheese and chopped chives. Spread the mixture on to the slices of bread, garnish with freshly ground black pepper, and serve.

PER SERVING: 200 kcal • 17 g protein • 3 g fat • 23 g carbohydrate

Tuna cream on

serve on small whole grain rolls for an ideal appetizer

whole grain toast

Serves 2: • 1 can of tuna in water (150 g (6 oz) drained) • juice from 1/2 lemon • 2 tbsp low-fat quark • salt • pepper • 4 slices whole grain toast • 4 radishes • 2 tbsp cress

Thoroughly drain the tuna in a sieve, then use a blender to purée the tuna finely with the lemon juice and quark. Add salt and pepper to the mixture. Toast the whole grain bread and spread with the mixture. Wash and slice the radishes and arrange on top of the tuna cream. Garnish with cress and serve.

PER SERVING: 205 kcal • 22 g protein • 13 g fat • 21 g carbohydrate

Fennel and

topped with rye breadcrumbs

pineapple

Mix the quark with the lime juice and milk and stir until smooth. Season with salt and pepper. Wash, peel, and trim the fennel bulb, then cut into strips. Set aside some of the fennel leaves.

Mix the fennel strips with the quark mixture. Peel the pineapple, taking care to remove any remnants of the skin. Cut the pineapple into quarters lengthways and remove the hard inner core. Dice the pineapple, but do not add to the fennel mixture until shortly before serving. Pineapple contains the enzyme bromelain, which causes a bitter taste when mixed with dairy products. Make breadcrumbs from the rye bread and sprinkle them over the fennel and pineapple mixture. Garnish with fennel leaves and serve.

Serves 2:
2 tbsp low-fat quark
juice from 1/2 lime
1–2 tbsp milk
salt
coloured pepper
1 small fennel bulb
half a small pineapple (200 g (7 oz))
2 slices rye bread

Fennel

As well as its fresh aniseed smell, fennel offers active a variety of highly valuable nutrients, such as vitamins A and E, calcium, and potassium. Buy small bulbs, since the larger bulbs have tough outer leaves that must be peeled.

PER SERVING:

141 kcal

5 g protein

1 g fat

26 g carbohydrate

power

Swordfish and mango goulash

exotic and an ideal source of energy

Bring 300 ml (3/4 pt) of lightly salted water to a boil. Wash the rice, then add it to the boiling water, cover tightly, and simmer for 30–40 minutes. Peel and chop the onions. Cut the swordfish into 1.5 cm (3/4 in) cubes. Peel the mango half, remove the stone, and dice. Blanch the peach and remove the skin. Then cut the peach in half, remove the stone, and cut the peach into wedges.

Heat the peanut oil in a deep non-stick pan and sauté the onions over a low heat until golden brown. Add the diced fish and sauté, turning constantly. Add the stock, stir in the mustard, and simmer for 5 minutes over a low heat. Season with salt and pepper. Add the fruit and heat for 2–3 minutes. Mix the cornflour with the cream, add to the goulash, and bring to the boil again briefly to thicken. Serve with the rice.

Serves 2:

150 g (6 oz) brown rice
1 small onion
300 g (12 oz) swordfish (slices or fillets)
1/2 mango
1 peach
2 tbsp peanut oil
250 ml (1/2 pt) vegetable or fish stock
1 tbsp hot mustard
pepper
salt
1 tsp cornflour
2 tbsp cream

Nutritious fish
You can also use any other firm white fish in this dish – halibut, for example. A crusty baguette or a serving of pasta make tasty alternatives to brown rice.

PER SERVING:

751 kcal

38 g protein

29 g fat

83 g carbohydrate

Herb-coated
with green beans and potatoes
pike-perch fillet

Drizzle the lemon juice over the pike-perch fillet, cover, and leave to stand for 10 minutes. Preheat the oven to 200°C (400°F). Wash and peel the potatoes and cut into chips. Wash and trim the beans, then simmer in a generous amount of water with the potatoes until al dente.

Serves 2:
300 g (12 oz) pike-perch fillet
juice of 1/2 lemon
300 g (12 oz) potatoes
300 g (12 oz) green beans
4 cloves garlic
40 g (2 oz) butter (at room temperature)
3 tbsp chopped parsley
20 g (1 oz) breadcrumbs
salt
pepper
2 tbsp chopped savory
2 tbsp freshly grated parmesan

Peel and crush the cloves of garlic. Mix the garlic with 30 g (1 oz) of the butter, the parsley, breadcrumbs, salt, and pepper. Brush the pike-perch fillet with this herb butter and bake in an oven-proof pan in the middle of the oven for 12–15 minutes, until crispy.

Drain the beans and potatoes. Melt the remaining butter, add the savory, and toss with the beans and potatoes.

Arrange the fish on a plate with a portion of the vegetables on the side, sprinkle with parmesan, and serve.

Pike-perch

This particularly fine freshwater fish contains generous amounts of vitamin D, iodine, and selenium. With only 0.7 g of fat per 100 g (4 oz), it is practically fat free. Like vitamin E – a very important vitamin for athletes – selenium is an antioxidant. Selenium protects the cells from cancer-causing free radicals.

PER SERVING:

506 kcal

41 g protein

21 g fat

38 g carbohydrate

power

Leek-wrapped
particularly rich in omega-3 fatty acids
salmon steaks

Trim the leek. Remove four of the outer leaves and set aside. Cut the leek in half lengthways and wash thoroughly, then slice crossways into half rings. Preheat the oven to 200°C (400°F). Bring a generous amount of salted water to the boil and boil the four leek leaves you set aside for 5 minutes. Use a slotted spoon to remove the leaves and drain them. Add the vermicelli to the boiling leek water and cook until al dente according to the directions on the packet. Cut the yellow pepper in half, remove the stem, seeds, and inner membranes, wash, and cut into strips. Heat the oil in a non-stick pan. Briefly sauté the leek and the pepper strips over a medium heat. Mix the soured cream and the crème fraîche, season with salt and pepper, and stir into the vegetables. Once the vermicelli is cooked, tip it into a colander and drain thoroughly. Then mix the pasta with the vegetables and pour into a casserole dish. Season the salmon steaks, then wrap each steak in two of the blanched leek leaves. "seam" side down on top of the vermicelli. Dot with flakes of butter, cover, and bake in the middle of the oven for 20 minutes.

Serves 2:

2 salmon steaks (150 g (6 oz) each)

1 large leek (approx. 250 g (10 oz) trimmed)

200 g (8 oz) vermicelli

1 yellow pepper

1 tbsp olive oil

4 tbsp soured cream

2 tbsp crème fraîche

salt

pepper

10 g (1/2 oz) butter

power

PER SERVING: 886 kcal • 47 g protein • 40 g fat • 83 g carbohydrate

Linguine with smoked catfish and basil

sophisticated fare even for athletic guests

Bring at least 2 litres (4 pts) of salted water to the boil and cook the linguine until al dente. Peel the shallots and garlic. Dice the shallots finely. Chop the capers.

Serves 2:
200 g (8 oz) linguine
2 shallots
1 clove garlic
2 tsp capers
2 tsp butter
50 ml (2 fl oz) vegetable stock
100 g (4 oz) crème fraîche
100 g (4 oz) smoked catfish
lemon juice
salt
pepper
2 tbsp chopped basil

For the sauce, heat the butter in a non-stick pan and sauté the shallots over a low heat until translucent. Crush the garlic and add it to the onions, then pour in the vegetable stock. Stir the capers and the crème fraîche into the broth.

When the linguine is cooked, pour into a colander and drain. Shred the smoked catfish, add to the sauce, and cook over a low heat. Season to taste with lemon juice, salt, and pepper, then stir in the linguine. Garnish with basil and capers and serve.

Catfish

The firm flesh of farmed catfish is particularly healthy, since they are fed on corn germ, wheat, and soya beans. You can substitute smoked trout fillet for the smoked catfish in this recipe.

PER SERVING:

796 kcal

39 g protein

31 g fat

88 g carbohydrate

power

Turkey schnitzel

rich in minerals thanks to wild rice and asparagus

in coconut milk

Bring 450 ml (1 pt) salted water to a boil. Wash the rice and add to the boiling water. Cover and simmer over a low heat for 35–40 minutes. Season the turkey schnitzels, then cut into thin strips. Peel the lower third of the asparagus stalks, then slice them diagonally into 3 cm (1.5 in) pieces. Peel the pineapple, discard the hard core, and cut into cubes. Cut open the chilli pepper, remove the seeds, and dice finely.

Heat the oil. Brown the turkey strips in the oil over medium heat. Add the asparagus and cook for 3–5 minutes, stirring constantly. Add the coconut milk, chilli paste, and diced chilli pepper and simmer over a low heat for 6 minutes. Dissolve the arrowroot in a little water and stir in. Add the pineapple and cook until heated through. Serve with wild rice.

Serves 2:
150 g (6 oz) wild rice
300 g (12 oz) turkey schnitzel
200 g (8 oz) green asparagus
1/2 pineapple (about 250 g (10 oz))
1/2 red chilli pepper
1 tbsp corn germ oil
400 ml (3/4 pt) coconut milk
1 tsp chilli paste
salt
white pepper
3 tsp arrowroot

Wild rice

Wild rice is actually the seed of American or Asian water grasses. It contains more protein, potassium, and magnesium than normal rice and should be a regular part of an athlete's diet, even though it is somewhat expensive. You can also buy wild rice mixed with other types of rice.

PER SERVING:

897 kcal

53 g protein

27 g fat

106 g carbohydrate

power

Chicken breast and apricot ragout

with bananas and basmati rice

Cook the rice in 300 ml (1/2 pt) salted water, covered, over low heat for 12–15 minutes until all the water has been absorbed. Then stir the rice and leave uncovered to let the steam escape.

Cut the chicken breast into narrow strips, then season with salt and pepper and sprinkle with the curry powder. Peel and chop the ginger. Cut the chilli pepper in half lengthways, remove the seeds, wash, and dice finely.

Heat the oil in a deep non-stick pan. Brown the chicken strips, ginger, and chilli pepper over a medium heat, stirring occasionally. Add the chicken stock and simmer over a low heat for 3 minutes.

Peel the banana and cut into thin slices. Wash the apricots, remove the stones, and cut into thin wedges. Add the banana, apricots, and raisins to the chicken mixture, stir, and heat for 2–3 minutes. Arrange the rice on two plates, top with the ragout, and serve.

Serves 2:
150 g (6 oz) basmati rice
300 g (12 oz) chicken breast
1 tbsp Madras curry powder
1 hazelnut-sized piece of ginger root
1/2 chilli pepper
2 tbsp peanut oil
200 ml (8 fl oz) chicken stock
1 banana
5 apricots
2 tbsp raisins
salt
pepper

Apricots – super-nutritious

Apricots are rich in potassium, silicic acid, B-vitamins, and carotinoids, making them a powerhouse of nutrition. The same applies to dried apricots – a good reason to nibble on dried fruit instead of sweets when you feel like a snack.

PER SERVING:

780 kcal

43 g protein

17 g fat

100 g carbohydrate

power

Pork fillet in

ideal for guests ... an exotic dish with aromatic rice

persimmon sauce

Trim the sinews from the pork fillet, then season with salt and pepper. Heat the sesame oil in a non-stick pan. Brown the fillet on all sides over medium heat for about 20 minutes. Wash the rice and cook with the raisins in double its volume of salted water for 10 minutes. Cut the chilli pepper in half lengthways, remove the seeds, wash and dice finely. Peel the persimmon, cut in half, remove the seeds, and dice finely. Dissolve the agar agar in the vegetable stock.

Once the pork fillet is browned, remove it from the pan and wrap it in aluminum foil to keep it warm. Briefly sauté the chilli pepper and persimmon in the pork juices, add the vegetable stock, and simmer over a low heat until the sauce is reduced. Use a large ladle to dish out a scoop of rice on each plate. Cut the meat in diagonal slices and arrange next to the rice. Pour the sauce over the meat and serve.

Serves 2:

1 small pork fillet (approx. 250 g (10 oz))
2 tbsp sesame oil
150 g (6 oz) aromatic Thai rice
2 tbsp raisins
1/2 chilli pepper
1 persimmon
1 tsp agar agar
250 ml (1/2 pt) vegetable stock
salt
pepper

Persimmons – food of the gods

Persimmons are an exotic, orange fruit, with an easily digestible soft, jelly-like flesh. They are rich in beta carotene and vitamin C.
If desired, you can substitute half a small, fresh pineapple (about 200 g (8 oz)) for the persimmon in this recipe.

PER SERVING:

576 kcal

33 g protein

12 g fat

80 g carbohydrate

Green beans

spicy and aromatic and loaded with minerals

with fillet steak

Peel and dice the onion, garlic, and ginger. Remove the seeds from the chilli pepper, then wash and dice finely. Trim the leek, cut in half lengthways, wash thoroughly, and then slice crossways into half rings. Trim and wash the beans.

Serves 2:

1 small onion

3 cloves garlic

1 hazelnut-sized piece of ginger root

1 green chilli pepper

1 leek

500 g (1 lb) green beans

2 tbsp rapeseed oil

1 tbsp raw cane

400 ml (3/4 pt) beef stock

2 small fillet steaks

salt

pepper

4 tbsp soured cream

1 tbsp cornflour

Heat 1 tbsp rapeseed oil in a deep, non-stick pan. Sauté the onions, garlic, ginger, and chilli pepper. Sprinkle with the sugar and continue to stir until melted. Add the beef stock, leek, and green beans, cover, and simmer for about 10 minutes over a low heat.

Using the flat side of a large knife, firmly press the steaks and season with salt and pepper. Heat the remaining oil in a non-stick pan and brown the steaks for 4 minutes on each side. Season the green beans. Mix the soured cream and cornflour together, stir into the vegetables, and leave to stand briefly. Arrange on a plate next to the steaks.

▶ **Green vegetables and meat**

The combination of green vegetables and meat guarantees excellent iron absorption. In the human body, red blood cells are up to 70 per cent iron, and iron is responsible for the transportation of oxygen in the blood. This dish also contains 161 mg magnesium and 1757 mg potassium, which represent a large percentage of the recommended daily allowance of these minerals.

PER SERVING:

483 kcal

41 g protein

23 g fat

28 g carbohydrate

power

Roast beef with
spicy and rich in magnesium
red lentils

Peel and chop the shallots. Heat 1 tbsp olive oil in a non-stick pan and sauté the shallots over a low heat until golden brown. Wash the lentils and add to the shallots. Add the beef stock. Cook the lentils over a low heat for 8–10 minutes until almost done.

In the meantime, cut the roast beef into strips. Heat the remaining oil in a non-stick pan and brown the roast beef strips over a medium heat until crispy.

Stir the chopped chives into the yogurt, then season with salt and pepper. Season the lentils with the raspberry vinegar and add to the roast beef. Arrange on two plates, with a topping of 1 tbsp of the chive yogurt. Serve the remaining sauce in a separate dish.

Serves 2:

2 shallots

2 tbsp olive oil

200 g (8 oz) red lentils

400 ml (3/4 pt) beef broth

150 g (6 oz) thinly sliced roast beef

150 g (6 oz) low-fat yogurt

4 tbsp chopped chives

salp

pepper

2 tbsp raspberry vinegar

Lentils

100 g (4 oz) lentils contain 129 mg magnesium and 840 mg potassium. In other words, when you eat a dish containing lentils, you have already had over one-third of the recommended daily allowance for magnesium. The same holds true for canned lentils. Red lentils are particularly quick to prepare, cooking in about 10 minutes.

PER SERVING:

534 kcal

45 g protein

4 g fat

58 g carbohydrate

power

Spaghetti and

rich in iron and magnesium

courgettes with steak

Bring at least 2 litres (4 pts) salted water to the boil and cook the spaghetti until al dente. Peel the courgette, then, using a vegetable peeler, cut it lengthways into 2 cm (1 in) wide strips. Peel and dice the shallot. Peel the garlic.

Serves 2:
100 g (4 oz) spaghetti
1 courgette (about 300 g (12 oz))
1 shallot
2–3 cloves garlic
2 steak fillets (150 g (6 oz) each)
salt
pepper
2 tbsp olive oil
2 tsp oregano
2 tbsp soured cream

Using the flat side of a large knife, press the steak fillets firmly and season with salt and pepper. Heat the oil in a non-stick pan. Brown the steaks in the pan over a medium heat for about 4–5 minutes per side until medium or well done. Wrap the steaks in aluminum foil to keep warm. Drain the spaghetti thoroughly in a colander.

Briefly sauté the shallot in the meat juices. Add the courgette strips and crushed garlic, season with oregano, and sauté until transparent, stirring constantly. Stir in the soured cream and spaghetti and arrange on plates with the steaks.

Courgette blossoms

The large, female blossoms grow attached to a small courgette and are suitable for filling. You can use the small male blossoms as edible decorations for pasta dishes and salads. Courgette blossoms are a good source of beta carotene, potassium, and calcium.

PER SERVING:

515 kcal

41 g protein

19 g fat

45 g carbohydrate

Carrot and spinach

a good source of potassium and vitamin E

pancake

Peel and wash the potatoes. Trim and peel the carrots. Using a large grater, grate the potatoes and carrots. Peel the onion and chop finely. Sort through and wash the fresh spinach, removing any large stems, then cut into strips and steam in a pan over medium heat until the spinach ceases to release water. If using frozen spinach, thaw it according to the instructions and press out any water. Mix the potatoes, carrots, onions, and spinach with the eggs. Season with black pepper and marjoram. Heat the oil in a flat, non-stick pan (25 cm (10 in) diameter). Add the vegetable batter, smooth, and cook for 20 minutes over a low heat. Turn over by gently sliding the pancake on to a large plate. Then, using a second plate, turn the pancake and carefully return it to the pan. Cook for another 10–15 minutes. Cut into pieces and serve. These pancakes go well with a fresh salad.

Serves 2:
400 g (1 lb) potatoes
100 g (4 oz) carrots
1 small onion
200 g (8 oz) fresh spinach (or 125 g (5 oz) frozen spinach)
2 eggs
black pepper
2 tbsp chopped marjoram
2 tbsp rapeseed oil

Potatoes and eggs

The protein in potatoes is particularly well utilized by the body. When combined with eggs, the protein is even more valuable than protein derived from meat. Potatoes are rich in potassium. Use salt sparingly since salt contains sodium, which impairs the positive effects of potassium.

PER SERVING:

300 kcal

13 g protein

15 g fat

27 g carbohydrate

power

Potato and
easy to prepare
beefburger casserole

Preheat the oven to 200°C (400°F). Peel and wash the potatoes, then use a vegetable peeler to cut into very thin slices. Lightly cut a cross into the top of the tomatoes and blanch for a few seconds in boiling water. Then slide off the skin and cut into slices. Wash the watercress, remove the stems, drain well, and chop.

Heat the oil in a non-stick pan. Break up the beefburger and brown over a high heat. Season with salt and pepper. Stir in the tomato purée, then leave the pan to one side. Drain the mozzarella and cut into slices.

Lightly oil a casserole dish and layer with half of the potatoes. Add one half of the beefburger mixture, then a layer of watercress. Add the remaining potatoes, followed by the remaining beefburger. Top with the tomato slices and then with the mozzarella slices.

Mix the egg with the milk and the cinnamon. Pour the milk mixture over the casserole. Bake in the middle of the oven for about 55 minutes until the potatoes are tender. If necessary, cover with aluminum foil to prevent the mozzarella from browning too much. Leave to stand for 5 minutes before serving.

Serves 2:
500 g (1lb 4 oz) potatoes
4 vine-ripened tomatoes
(approx. 400 g (1 lb))
50 g (2 oz) watercress
1 tbsp rapeseed oil
250 g (10 oz) beefburger
salt
pepper
2 tbsp tomato purée
125 g (5 oz) mozzarella
oil for the casserole dish
1 egg
100 ml (4 fl oz) low-fat milk
1 tsp cinnamon

power

PER SERVING: 565 kcal • 50 g protein • 22 g fat • 40 g carbohydrate

Gnocchi with oyster mushrooms

a fast and easy source of minerals

Cook the gnocchi in lots of salted water, according to the directions on the packet. Trim the shallot and dice finely. Cut the ham into thin strips. Trim and wash the oyster mushrooms, then cut into strips.

Heat the butter in a deep non-stick pan. Add the shallot and ham and brown over a medium heat. Add the oyster mushrooms and sauté for 3–4 minutes over a low heat, stirring constantly.

Drain the cooked gnocchi in a colander. Add the cream and milk to the mushrooms, then season to taste with salt and pepper. Reduce the cream over a low heat for 1–2 minutes. Stir the parmesan and gnocchi into the mushrooms. Arrange the gnocchi on plates, garnish with chives, and serve immediately.

Serves 2:

400 g (1 lb) fresh gnocchi

1 shallot

100 g (4 oz) lean cooked ham

200 g (8 oz) oyster mushrooms

1 tbsp butter

3 tbsp cream

100 ml (4 fl oz) low-fat milk

salt

black pepper

2 tbsp freshly grated parmesan

2 tbsp chopped chives

Mushrooms

Mushrooms are rich in potassium, and also contain some magnesium and iron. Some types are rich in niacin, a nutrient that plays an important role in energy conversion. You should only buy mushrooms that are firm and dry. Prepare mushrooms on the same day you buy them since they lose many of their nutrients when they are stored.

PER SERVING:

390 kcal

20 g protein

20 g fat

31 g carbohydrate

Index

For Athletes: Fitness Food

INDEX

> **Abbreviations**
> tsp = teaspoon
> tbsp= tablespoon

Imprint

First published in the UK by
Gaia Books Ltd, 20 High Street,
Stroud, GL5 1AZ
www.gaiabooks.co.uk

Registered at 66 Charlotte St,
London W1T 4QE
Originally published under the title
Fitness Food

© Gräfe und Unzer Verlag GmbH
Munich. English translation copyright
© 2001 Gaia Books Ltd
Translated in association with
Silverback Books, Inc. USA

Editorial: Katherine Pate

Nutrition advisor: Angela Dowden

Reproduction: MRM Graphics Ltd,
Winslow, UK.
Printed in Singapore

ISBN 1 85675 167 8

A catalogue record for this book is available in
the British Library

10 9 8 7 6 5 4 3 2 1

Caution
The techniques and recipes in this book
are to be used at the reader's sole
discretion and risk.
Always consult a doctor if you are in doubt
about a medical condition.

Doris Muliar
born in Austria, Muliar has worked for the radio,
television, and publishing industries since 1985
and concentrates her efforts in the field of
health. She loves to cook as a hobby and
specializes in low-fat foods. Since she is also very
active, she knows how she can achieve optimal
fitness and performance by eating a low-fat diet.

Susie M. and **Pete Eising** have studios in
Munich, Germany, and Kennebunkport, Maine,
in the United States. They studied at the
Fachakademie für Fotodesign in Munich, where
they founded their own studio for food
photography in 1991.

For this book:
Photographic layout:
Martina Görach
Food styling:
Monika Schuster

We would like to thank the following for their
support during photo production:
Sabre (Paris)
LSA (London)
Christiane Perrochon (Capannole, Italy)
Michael Aram (New Jersey)
Sompex (Meerbusch)

FENG SHUI COOKING
Recipes for harmony and health
Fahrnow, Fahrnow, and Sator
£4.99
ISBN 1 85675 146 5
More energy and wellbeing
from recipes that balance
your food.

BEAUTY FOOD
The natural way to looking good
Dagmar von Cramm
£4.99
ISBN 1 85675 141 4
Natural Beauty for skin and
hair - eating routines for a
fabulous complexion.

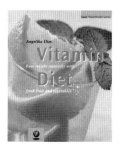

VITAMIN DIET
Lose weight naturally with fresh
fruit and vegetables
Angelika Ilies
£4.99
ISBN 1 85675 145 7
All the benefits of eating fresh
fruit and vegetables plus a
natural way to weight loss.

LOW CHOLESTEROL - LOW FAT
The easy way to reduce
cholesterol, stay slim and
enjoy your food
Döpp, Willrich and Rebbe
£4.99
ISBN 1 85675 166 X
Stay fit, slim and healthy
with easy-to-prepare
gourmet feasts.

ENERGY DRINKS
Power-packed juices, mixed,
shaken or stirred
Friedrich Bohlmann
£4.99
ISBN 1 85675 140 6
Fresh juices packed full of
goodness for vitality and
health.

ANTI STRESS
Recipes for acid-alkaline balance
Dagmar von Cramm
£4.99
ISBN 1 85675 155 4
A balanced diet to reduce
stress levels, maximise
immunity and help you
keep fit.

DETOX
Foods to cleanse and purify
from within
Angelika Ilies
£4.99
ISBN 1 85675 150 3
Detoxify your body as part of
your daily routine by eating
nutritional foods that have
cleansing properties.

MOOD FOOD
Recipes to cheer you up,
revitalize and comfort you
Marlisa Szwillus
£4.99
ISBN 1 85675 161 9
The best soul comforters,
the quickest revitalizers
and the most satisfying
stress busters.

To order the books featured on this page call 01453 752985, fax 01453 752987 with your credit/debit card details, or
send a cheque made payable to Gaia Books to Gaia Books Ltd., 20 High Street, Stroud, Glos., GL5 1AZ.
e-mail: gaiapub@dircon.co.uk or visit our website www.gaiabooks.co.uk